SENT TO FORGIVE

Art By Gerald

Helen E. Hansen

Sent To Forgive

Helen E. Hansen

Dear Reader, I wish to tell you that I feel it is a privilege for me to share my story with you.

I cannot speak to the world's tragedies — only to my own little life's events — an unimaginable journey of hatred and forgiveness that has lifted me, finally, to a peace I cannot adequately describe.

I was 600 miles away from home when I learned my son had been murdered.

Seeing my mother through surgery at the Portland hospital, I phoned Kristine that evening to tell her that her grandmother's surgery was over. My daughter was barely able to reply, her voice broken into sobs and crying. Something about the police having just left... or the coroner — they'd come to her house to tell her that John had been shot, murdered, where he was sleeping.

I struggled to make sense of what she was saying. John had been camping near the Feather River and was shot in the head as he slept in his sleeping bag. As the meaning of her words began to sink in, everything went gray and numb.

What must I do? What can I do? Mother was diabetic and her cataract surgery had not gone well. I must stay here. But I must go home — my children need me there. I had to find a way to tell Mother that I would not be able to stay with her. We called her doctor and her minister; together they told her of the tragedy. Was it this news that was responsible for a setback in her condition? She was kept in the hospital as I flew home on a ticket arranged by my oldest son Larry.

Home, but how different it was. This unthinkable event had brought all my children together again. Karl, my second son, had just arrived from San Luis Obispo, and left again to make the sorrowful trip to Marysville to identify his brother's body.

Was it only a year ago we were gathered just like this, mourning the loss of my dearly beloved husband, their father, to a sudden heart attack? It didn't seem possible.

There was no time for dealing with the grief. It was held at bay by all of us as we kept our attention on making immediate funeral arrangements, trying to imagine what John would have wanted had he been able to anticipate his own premature departure. Representatives of the Marysville Police Department and Coroners Office, with their courteous but insistent questions, would not allow us a moment of forgetting. Calling friends and relatives to inform them of what we had no words for, answering phone calls from loved ones who did not know what to say to us. Our little family moved through the scene like zombies. None of us dared to voice our pain or could even begin to find the words.

The funeral passed in a haze of faces before me, condolences were heard as hushed, half-finished phrases. What could they say? I was grateful to have to return to Portland to bring Mother home from the hospital and keep her as the focus of my attention for the next month. The mind is a wonderful thing. Day by day I was able to set aside my own memories and concentrate on the care Mother needed. As soon as medically possible, I brought her back to Sacramento to stay with me. Only through the strength of my Lord and the many who remembered me in their prayers was I sustained.

By the time Mother returned to her home, everyone assumed that I was well on the road to accommodate my loss. If only that were possible! Time ground to a standstill. Days and nights blurred together without meaning.

I only knew that my body ached terribly, as if all the grief had settled into every muscle, every joint, and deep down into my bones. It took all my energy to will to get up from bed and move to the chair, knowing that each step exacted great pain.

The overwhelming loneliness weighed me down. I missed my husband so much — his strength, his caring. He and John both were taken away so abruptly, no time to say good-bye, I will always love you. Friends fell away, embarrassed by my pain. They could understand someone's long-term bout with cancer or long-term rehab for an amputation. But they do not treat someone left behind by death in the same way. Society demands that survivors hurry up, get involved in some work, something therapeutic, and get on with their lives. They do not wish to be upset by one who is outwardly grieving.

But a broken heart, though invisible, will not let its owner go.

I was held in a kind of disconnection. Schedules and patterns of eating, sleeping, reading, and doing errands all dissolved in a loss of purpose. Long, long hours. A disbelief that I would never see John again. Why? Why? The Marysville police had provided the grim details of John's murder. At 5:30 on that morning, Gerald Mann happened on the campsite where John was sleeping and shot him in the head with a .32 caliber pistol. Mann was frightened away by a passing motorcyclist while rifling my dead son's pockets. John was 28, Mann was 23. He was arrested just a few days later.

Gerald Eugene Mann had been a very troubled young man. After pleading guilty to a kidnap charge involving the abduction of a 26-year-old woman at knifepoint, he was declared a mentally disordered sex offender and sent to Atascadero State Hospital. Released on probation four years later, this psychopath/sociopath (someone who is aggressively anti-social) was living "out of his car" and with relatives. Only a few months later, at the time of his arrest, he was charged not only with my son's murder, but with ten additional major felonies, including kidnapping, rape, burglary and armed robbery. Why had they let this monster free? How had he happened on to John's campsite? Why did he shoot a man asleep who was no threat to him? Why?

Grieving is a living hell with its unanswerable WHYs.

I moved as an empty shell, the weight of my venomous hatred constricting my breath and canceling any ability to reason. Where were the friends I had counted most dear? Withdrawn. Refusing to listen. Leaving me alone as memories of my lost son returned to ache my heart.

John, such a happy little boy, always singing. Like his father, gifted musically, perfect pitch. Even as a kindergartner, walking home from school, John would see our home at the bottom of the hill and sing all the way down.

And he was so creative. I remember one of his first works of mosaic tile: a background of deep cobalt to light sea blue, with the brown sea floor holding green sea plants swaying in the current. Two fish in the center — a small unsuspecting gold fish, followed closely by a large yellow fish with gaping jaws. "See this little fish, Mom? Well, that's me, and one day the big fish will swallow me up." I did not know what he meant.

He was a gentle young man, drawn to exploring mountains and learning how they were formed, propelling him into a geology major in college.

But Vietnam cut that short. Selective Service called John's number and off he went to war. A terrible war. A war that changed John, robbing him of his life's song. He was crushed by war's devastation. He came back changed, restless, hurt by the personal rejection he received here, even from former friends. The nation he had served had closed their hearts against the returning veterans. How as parents we tried to make our children whole again. But who could heal the deep spiritual wounding of warfare, wounds that drugs and alcohol only briefly numb.

John planned to go back to college and take up his Junior year geology coursework where he had left off, but he could not seem to shake the dark sadness that he had brought back from Vietnam; he found concentration difficult and decided maybe he'd work for awhile. And then his father had a fatal heart attack. For all of us this was unexpected and heartbreaking. For John it was devastating. He took off on a camping trip, a trip we all hoped would help him sort out his pain and find peace. His travels took him as far as Wyoming, seeking healing in his beloved Nature. Then, after several weeks, he was on his way home again, camping one last night near Marysville, the last night of his life.

As the time for Gerald Mann's trial approached, the Chief Trial Deputy kept our family informed, returning our calls, letting us know about court dates and time schedules. He understood that every trip I made to Marysville was an emotionally exhausting, 50-mile trek.

Each time I sat in the courtroom, I had to remind myself that as the survivor of a murdered victim, I had no rights in court. I would be allowed to stay only if I sat quietly, showed no emotion, caused no problems. Sit without response when I first saw the man who had murdered my son. Express no emotion as the psychiatrist recounted Mann's motive, in his own words: "I didn't give it much thought as to why I killed him. He was just there." Sit quietly as the officer testified that Mann was apprehended through the testimony of the 15-year-old girl he had abducted and raped the day following John's murder. The only concern of the judicial system was the defendant. The Judge continually used the term "son" when speaking to Gerald Mann, extending to him the concern of the court. Every care was taken to be sure that he understood each decision and ruling the court made, to guarantee a fair trial.

The pain of sitting in that courtroom listening to the coroner detail the murder of my beloved son! John's body was found at rest, as though sleeping. The campsite was neat and orderly. No drugs or alcohol were found at autopsy…the body was clean. He was lying on his back, with one hand across his face, palm upward, cupping a pool of blood from his nose. The bullet had entered through the back of the head and lodged in his brain. There was no evidence of a struggle. Only a small, empty milk carton near the body.

Each day as my son's murderer was led into the courtroom, wrists cuffed and ankles manacled, surrounded by police. Security had been reinforced when a jail informant said that Mann intended to grab a deputy's gun and shoot his way out. He was counting on this futile act to guarantee a kind of "suicide by cop," this man who, the night before the trial, had told his attorney, "Yeah I did it all, and a lot of other stuff they don't know about. I saw this man sleeping. I shot him. I felt his pulse. I knew he was dead, and I felt good."

During the hearing, I was taking notes in a small notebook. Survivors of murdered victims must gather their own information about what had happened — there is no advocate to assist them. The judge sent his bailiff to where I was sitting. What purpose did I have in being in court, he asked. Why was I taking notes? Was I Gerald Mann's mother?

I assured him I was not Gerald Mann's mother. I was John's mother.

"Who is John?" he asked.

"The one who was murdered!" I replied with some anguish.

The judge asked to see the notebook, scanned the pages, and returned it to the bailiff. He instructed me that I was to cease from taking notes while court was in session; when court was concluded he would advise me how I could get a copy of the transcript (which I found out later costs from $100 to $300). I subscribed to the daily newspaper, The Marysville *Appeal-Democrat,* as an alternative source of information for the months that Gerald Mann was in court. Today, victims of survivors do have rights, but it took long hours of legislative debate to assure that the courts understand: victims are a part of the reason the court is in session. So I sat, day after day, in silence, my blood cold, my spirit numb, empty, emotionless.

The day before the Superior Court started impaneling the jurors, Mann told his attorney to enter his plea: guilty by reason of insanity. With infinite patience, the judge explained to the accused that if he were to plead guilty to all the crimes, and then be judged sane by the two court-appointed psychiatrists, there would be no further recourse to a trial. Mann said he understood. Both psychiatrists found him sane — aware of what he was doing at the time he committed his crimes. The judge proceeded directly to the sentencing.

Gerald Mann was found guilty and given three consecutive life sentences for ten major felony counts. As soon as he finishes one sentence, even allowing time off for good behavior, he will move immediately to the next one. This means a minimum of 4o+ years before parole is even considered. I do not believe in the death penalty. One death plus one death does not equal the life of my son.

On this day of sentencing, I believed I would never have to see Gerald Mann again. Never have to face newspaper and television crews taking continuous pictures — asking how I felt when I heard my child had been murdered.

The trial was over. The Deputy Trial Attorney took me into his office, expressing his concern for the family and our loss. The sergeant returned my son's empty wallet, saying how he wished he could give me back my son instead.

I walked out of the courthouse, mechanically stopping at the street corner, words of suppressed rage screaming inside — WHY! He didn't even know him! Where was God! Why was this madman allowed back into society? Why.

Silence was the only answer.

How to find a reason to continue living. So much advice from people so willing to be helpful:

"All that's happened is in the past. Why do you keep reliving it.
You're only making yourself sick."
"I know <u>exactly</u> how you feel...I know someone who..."
"You've got to stop carrying on like this and feeling sorry for yourself.
Think of others for a change."
"It was God's will."
"You're not the only one who's suffered like this."
"God must have loved John so much He wanted him to come to heaven to be with Him."
"You're not yourself anymore. You're making me feel depressed.
Call me when you get over it."

I returned home to face an intense emptiness, without knowing what to do next. And who cared anyway. If life can be so randomly cruel, why plan anything. What's the use in trying. John was gone — this was real — I would not see him again. A great black hole had opened inside me, as icy and unfathomable as the ones astronomers have found in deep space. It had settled within me, deeper than my bone marrow; it became a permanent part of who I now was.

I visited my children, trying to connect. Very few families are able to remain close in the face of this kind of tragedy. As each of us struggled to come to terms with John's loss, hurt and angry outbursts divided us one against another. After-shocks of the event itself kept us emotionally off balance.

I thought back to my childhood...I was blessed with a Christian heritage. I can't remember a time in my life when Sunday was not a day set apart for church and Sunday school. My grandfather was a circuit-riding Baptist minister for homestead families in central Oregon. I still have the leather saddlebag fashioned especially for him to hold his Bible and songbook. We grew up in Sunnyside Methodist Church, a faith community that the depression years bonded together in nurturing one another and their children. Memories are vivid of my mother and father working in every endeavor of that little stone church. They served on committees, bazaars, potlucks, and always in the Sunday school, always in the worship service. We children sitting all together in our little wooden chairs singing, "Jesus loves me, this I know, for the Bible tells me so." It was a simple time, an innocent time. Our faith and fellowship were sufficient for all our needs, and the line between right and wrong was never in doubt.

That all seemed so far away now. In my life of solitude I found my soul enraged – now in spiritual warfare with the God of my childhood. I read the Bible every day. I needed to know that God agreed with me — murder is an unforgivable sin — and found passages that affirmed justified retribution in the Psalms. I went to war using scripture to prove I was right.

Yet, for reasons I could not understand, God had retreated to the farthest reaches of the universe.

I spent nights crying in a grief that felt overpowering. I despaired for my life, longing to be free from this relentless sorrowing. With my faith completely shaken, my prayers took a dark turn.

Lord, make someone *else* the instrument of your peace!

Where there is hatred, I choose outrage.
Where there is injury, I remain paralyzed.
Where there is doubt, I cry out "WHY!"
Where there is despair, I embrace bitterness.
Where there is darkness, I hide in its void.
Where there is sadness, I sit in Job's ashes.

Within the space of just five years I had lost my husband, my son, my mother, and a dear friend who committed suicide.

In my darkest time, I prayed to die. I knew I could not take my own life, but oh how I prayed to be released. Dear God, if you hear me at all, I do not want to live! Please come in the night and take me home or wherever You send me. I've failed my family. I've failed You. Please take me. I can't endure another day.

But I did not die. For years I lived each day with clenched heart, clenched mind, and a clenched fist raised to heaven, imprisoned in my earth-bound soul. How I clung to that withering hatred!

My way out was not my doing but through unmerited Grace. I began hearing other voices crying. I slowly became aware of widows and children and fathers and babies, each alone and crying out, the whole world of sorrowing souls whose hearts had been crushed as mine had. The steps out of my depression were outward, towards those locked in their own grief struggle.

I helped facilitate a group called Parents of Murdered Children. There was a time in my life when I would have been appalled to think such a group existed; there are chapters all over America. The first meeting of the Sacramento chapter brought 17 of us together, sharing ten slain children. We sat close to one another in the living room of the host couple, feeling for the first time that we weren't alone anymore. We gave each other a sanctuary of safety, where rage, anguish, confusion, and pain could be freely expressed without embarrassment. And what a torrent of sorrow poured out! Such stories of children murdered in ways so violent the mind reeled.

The single most valuable thing we could do was simply to *listen*. That's the gift we gave one another, no advice, no therapy, no answers. Only those who have been through it themselves can be of help. When we said, "I know how you feel," we really did know.

It's not easy to sit in a group like this. Strong emotions of seemingly endless grief brought each mother and father to the edge of collapse. The loss of a child produced failed marriages, suicides. Some refused to be helped. There were some parents who wanted only revenge, bitter beyond Job's bitterness. The violent death of their son or daughter had shattered their belief in anything good or decent. Yet they continued to come to the meetings.

We shared, too, stories of the failure of every segment of our society to help us find a way of putting our lives back together. Friends turning away, unable to understand that we *wanted* to talk about this. Religious institutions unable to cope with our raw, God-condemning pleas. Ministers and clergy utterly at a loss at how to counsel. City and county officials treating us as just case numbers. The justice system seeming to support only the killers. Murderers going free on legal technicalities. A judge telling a victim's sister that, if he saw any more tears rolling down her cheek, he would send her out of the courtroom. It was ironic that one of our purposes as a group was to *educate the professionals* in how to help survivors in crisis.

It was after one such emotionally exhausting evening that I went to bed, completely spent. I fell into a sleep, deep and restful it seemed, into a dream that I was waking up in a strange new peace, waking to a new day bright with sunshine. I found myself walking down a wide pathway, feeling joy at hearing birds singing and delighting in the bright flowers that were brushed by the gentlest of warm breezes. The path led to the right, up a hill that towered high in the distance. On top of that hill was a temple of such unsurpassed beauty, I felt I had to go there. The pathway to climb was wide, inviting, lined with flowers, shaded by great trees whose boughs were filled with birds of all kinds singing. "This way. This way," they seemed to say.

I wanted to share this walk with others. I didn't want to walk it alone. There were strangers on the roadway — no one I knew — each walking alone. I called to each one, "It's such a beautiful day, come walk with me. It won't take us long to reach the top." But each stranger replied with only a shake of the head and continued their pace alone. One last stranger I called out to stopped for a moment. He looked up to the high mountain and said very softly, "That is a high journey. The way is not easy. To travel to Jerusalem, you must travel alone." I remembered that the name "Jerusalem" means "the place of peace."

The silent travelers somehow disappeared. I turned again to the path; it seemed a highway to heaven. I could see it wouldn't take long. The climb at first seemed easy, filled with bird-song and gracious sunlight.

Then unaccountably, the path started to narrow. The route to the top became less clear; confusing trails would become dead-ends or require that I take a detour. Each path I followed took me to the home of someone I had loved and lost, dear ones who had died and left me here. A sadness filled me as I remembered each one's special place in my life. I saw them, but I could not reach them. They were there, but they were absent. One little path led to John, but he could not see me. A cloud of darkness covered my vision, but my aching heart told me he was there.

Ominously, the pathway grew smaller, steeper, darker. I hiked to a high point to get my bearings. Had I taken a wrong turn? Where was the wide path, so clear, so inviting? Where was the Temple bidding me to come up? I looked out over a valley. I looked for my family, but everything had become blanketed in a fog of mist. Anxiously, I looked to the heights, but night had blacked it out completely. Searching around me — I could see no path! No here. No there. I was paralyzed by fear, fixed as if encased in stone. Crashing around me came thunder and lightning of a terrible storm. Terror stricken, I could not move as blinding rain swept over me. There was no escape!

I could feel the waters rising, soon to sweep me away. My tears and cries were useless. There was no one to hear, no one would find me. Trapped — abandoned — I resigned myself to inevitable death. It didn't seem to matter as I sank down into the cold soggy clay. Nothing mattered anymore and dying seemed easy.

Then a voice, a voice on the wind, calm yet so forceful, called me. "Helen, look up." I could barely see through the storm.

"Helen, take my hand. I'm reaching down to you."

I had no strength, but I reached up and felt my hand touching another. I was being pulled up...my mired feet were coming free...the cold stone of my prison was releasing me...releasing.

And I was drawn up to the top of the mountain, shivering with cold, mud-covered, bedraggled, I was drawn up and enfolded in a Love so healing, so compassionate, so cleansing. I could not see the face of my Savior, but I felt the tears being washed from my eyes. I didn't want to look up, afraid the enfolding Mystery might vanish. My heart started beating. New strength coursed all through me, healing, revitalizing, filling me entirely.

Then the voice spoke, a voice I knew as Love itself. It asked me to look again at the path I'd climbed. I looked, but the valley was still covered in misty clouds. The voice asked me to look at the other side of the mountain. I looked, but it too was obscured, its dark mystery was only more mysterious.

But searching more carefully through the mist, I began to see people scattered along the mountainside, sorrowing, lamenting, each one all alone. Far down I saw a gray wall where people were gathered to pray. They had wedged scraps of paper into the crevices, each paper recorded a broken heart. I saw such suffering - all exiles, all home-seeking, fallen in weariness. So many.

Then, above the mist, there appeared again the beautiful Temple Jerusalem. It seemed mostly dark now, with windows of slate gray, as if awaiting the Celestial Sun. Yet the temple gates stood open wide, beckoning, inviting all the weary, struggling pilgrims. And inside, bathed in sunlight, there stood a banquet table, laden with all good things, awaiting the guests' arrival.

I didn't understand what I was seeing. And I didn't want to leave Love's embrace. I was afraid of the suffering people I had seen, afraid to return to my own suffering.

The voice spoke again. It said not to be afraid, for I have never walked alone. It said that together we would walk down the mountain and heal everyone one the way. It said we must visit the wall and gather each precious paper, each tear. Then, when we had touched every hurting heart, we would all come up together to the Temple, we would enter the great hall, we would sit at the table, and know the fullness of Love that is our Creator.

That was the dream, but so much more than a dream. When I awoke, its impact remained with me.

It was the Spring of 1988 — a date I'll always remember. It started with a phone call from my friend Pat, inviting me to a series of four sessions that were being held at her church, Trinity Episcopal. The topic was "Centering Prayer". I agreed to go.

As I listened to the lectures, it seemed a strange kind of prayer to me, a prayer done in silent meditation. Nothing was spoken, no intercessions or requests made for God's favors. We were told to sit relaxed, in silence, with our minds at rest in the presence of God.

Strange, strange for this Baptist/ Lutheran/ Methodist who knew only the active way of praying. But my beginning attempts, in the company of other novices, brought a glimmer of peacefulness that I had never known before. I read *Open Mind, Open Heart* by Fr. Thomas Keating and listened to tape recordings by Father Basil Pennington, two Trappist monks who were bringing this practice from the monastery to share with laity of all faiths.

But back home, praying alone, I felt myself falling into a foreboding darkness. I pulled back. I can't do this, I thought. Alone there in the emptiness of my home, I sat crying, trying to understand why my attempts at Centering Prayer went wrong. Through my tears, I thumbed through Fr. Pennington's book, *A Retreat With Thomas Merton.* The text jumped into focus:

"And, I am scheduled to go to California in June…"

It was now late Spring. What year was this book written? Where in California would he come? I had no way to know.

The ringing telephone startled me. It was a voice I had not heard in a long time, my friend George, who said he wanted to check my address so he could send me a book. Thoughtfully, he asked me, "How are things going for you, Helen?" I tearfully told him of my disappointing encounter with Centering Prayer and what I had just read in Fr. Pennington's book. Did George know him? Was he was coming to California? And where? Had I missed him?

George did know. He said that in two months Father Pennington would be giving a retreat only 15 minutes from my home, at Christ the King Retreat Center! I stammered something about my not being Catholic and so probably I could not go there. But George assured me that I would be most welcome.

I hesitated. Should I? Could I? I called the retreat center and learned the dates. Seven days in a Catholic place, with the option of spending six nights there as well.

"I'm not a Catholic," I said to the receptionist.

"That doesn't matter," she said. "No one is excluded."

I made a reservation to attend the retreat. But after hanging up, every reason in the world not to go presented itself. How do I participate in this Catholic setting so I don't offend anyone? How could I pray with them when I knew none of their rituals? What would they think of me if they knew that I could no longer pray The Lord's Prayer — "…as we forgive those who trespass against us" — convinced that the act of murder could never be forgiven. But I so wanted to learn about this silent way of praying and its promise of peace.

My friend Myrna said she would be my safety net. If I felt that I needed to bail out of the retreat, she would drive out and bring me home. Besides, she said, you don't have to tell anyone you're not Catholic. It's not like it's stamped on your forehead.

Still, I hedged my bet. I would attend only during the day and come home at night. But Spirit was pushing me forward.

"You need to stay nights as well."

I called back and confirmed the full reservation. "You'll find it a much more meaningful retreat if you don't have to run back and forth," the receptionist assured me.

I would go, I would spend the nights there, but I firmly resolved to stay back in the shadows, not cause a stir, just quietly tag along. I would arrive early and take the chair in the circle that was closest to the exit door. But what happened! I was the <u>last</u> to arrive. To this day I can't figure out how that happened. I'm never late for anything! To my dismay, I saw that the only seat left was next to the retreat director, Father Pennington. I looked around for a stray chair that I could squeeze into a less conspicuous place. But Fr. Pennington waved me forward saying, "This place is for you." I stammered, "I didn't want to be at the head of the class." Everyone laughed, a warm, receptive laugh, and I sat down.

Father said that for our first gathering, we would simply use the time to get to know each other. He would begin teaching about Centering Prayer the next morning. But for tonight, each one of us had a story to tell and all the time we needed to tell it. We would each speak to two questions: what parish or faith community we belonged to and why we had set aside this week to come away to this retreat center. The exact two questions I had dreaded the most! How could I speak and still keep the secrets I had so carefully planned to hide?

Thankfully, Father said he would start with himself and then, moving to his left, we would go around the circle until everyone had spoken. That meant that I would be the very last one to share, but that was no comfort. What would I say? Could I possibly keep my over-burdened heart from speaking out? My hastily formulated strategy was to listen carefully to each person as they shared, and then, borrowing from their words, patch together my own offering.

I listened intently as they each told their own story. No two were alike, each had a song and a sorrow. But now it was my turn! My carefully prepared thoughts were pushed aside by words I could not keep back. My shell was breaking, my precautions were coming undone. I told of John's murder and the Lord's impossible command to forgive! In complete defiance of my earlier resolve I heard myself saying, "I'm not praying the prayer of forgiveness because I cannot understand it. My name is Helen Hansen... and I'm Lutheran. I've come here because I want my prayer to be made whole again. I want to learn Centering Prayer."

In a spontaneously loving gesture, those who had been listening gathered around me, enfolding me in their concern and caring, asking questions about what I had told them. Unexpected and beautiful new family! A stranger no longer.

My first night of the retreat, looking up at the crucifix that hung over my bed, I prayed silently, releasing my burden of hesitancy and doubt, asking only to abide here in this beautiful sanctuary of understanding.

The next day Father Pennington began his lessons on Centering Prayer. A very gentle teaching. Centering Prayer acknowledges that God is a loving Father who already knows our hearts, our needs, and our most profound fears. Really, there is no need for us to petition or beg a Father who wants only our complete well being and knows, better than we do, what is best for us. We need simply to come away to a quiet place, close the door to all outside distractions and interior anxieties, and give the only gift we can give God, our entire self.

God's language is silence. When we become still, content to simply sit in His Presence, we allow our loving Father to remind us that we are His children. Divine Life is the central core of every human being — it is the source of our inherent goodness. We allow His healing to reach us in Centering Prayer, as it never can in our frantic busy lives.

Because our minds generate thoughts ceaselessly, automatically, the Centering Prayer method does not say to try to suppress them (which is really impossible). When thoughts, sensations or feelings inevitably arise, we notice them and then return to our meditation. This is made easier by choosing a "sacred word", a small word like "love" or "peace" or "grace" that is quietly remembered when thoughts come up to bother us, a word we place gently in our consciousness as a sign of our intention to give ourselves to God. I chose "Jesus" as my sacred word.

As members of the retreat gathered to try this special prayer for ourselves, I felt so many loving friends surrounded me. With a sincere wish to be drawn closer to our loving Father, we closed our eyes, gifting each other with stillness. At times, random thoughts would whiz in and out, but gently remembering the sacred word was so simple and effective, I became less and less distracted.

Most miraculous of all, there is an inner stillness in all of us that this prayer gives us access to. The more time I gave to Centering Prayer, especially in a group, the closer I came to peace. Real peace. Something I would not have thought possible before.

I looked at the retreat schedule. To my dismay, we were all to receive Holy Eucharist each afternoon. What should I do? Would I be allowed to participate since, as a Lutheran, our Communion service was so different from Eucharist at Mass? Feeling like an outcast, but not wishing to offend the others, I approached Father Pennington. I said, "I'm a Lutheran. I know I can't share in Holy Eucharist. What should I do when the others go to Mass? Sit quietly in the back or should I stay in my room until Mass is over?"

Fr. Pennington replied with such gentleness, "Tell me the meaning the Lord's meal holds for you."

I struggled for words to convey the mystery of Communion; I answered that ever since the early years of my childhood, I believed that this sacred meal was nurturing me somehow.

"Come then," Fr. Pennington said, "you belong with us!"

What joy I felt at hearing this!

Within the retreat format, we had each been assigned a partner so that, two by two, we could deepen friendships. The grounds surrounding the Christ the King retreat center held beautiful pathways for quiet strolls. I asked my partner to explain the walkway marked: "Stations of the Cross." She said it was a special meditation that moved through the passion of Christ, pausing to remember each significant step leading to His crucifixion and death. With the help of a brochure thoughtfully provided by the center, we walked meditatively together through each of the fourteen stations.

I was so moved by the 13th station, the desolate mother Mary receives the body of her dead Son, I returned there later on my own. Quite unaccountably, no one else was there. I had the beautiful garden all to myself.

Lutherans don't pray to the Virgin Mary. Our church gives her no special recognition, except in Bible passages and Christmas pageants. But I was held in place there at the statue of Mary holding her Son, HER MURDERED SON. I heard a voice inside me saying,

"I understand your pain."

This resonated so deep within me, I found myself sobbing, not caring if anyone heard. Here was a mother like me. She knew a mother's agony for a murdered son. No one else could know the anguish of my heart, the frigid black hole of grief that was now my constant companion. She knew! And her message to me, spoken in just four words, opened my grief-bound heart.

On that afternoon, I embraced her as my Mother.

That night, I fell into a troubled sleep. Then, I was awakened — or was I still sleeping?

I really don't know how to explain it. The darkness of night was all around, and the darkness of my grieving filled my soul's interior. Into this darkness came a Light that suffused the room, bringing a warmth and serenity that were not of this world. A voice, not a voice, but more like a knowing, said clearly:

"Never has my Cup been turned away from you."

and then,

"My Cup has never been offered to Gerald Mann."

The Light was gone. The warmth was gone. Night returned. Only the words remained. I felt strangely quiet, as if suspended in silent space. The Light had left a sense of peace, but something in me anticipated a coming storm. The voice had spoken a name I never wanted to hear again, a name I had kept buried — the name of the man who had murdered my son.

When morning came, my distraught mind drove me to seek help to understand the meaning of the dream.

I asked Father Pennington if I could speak with him for a moment. He suggested that I come to his apartment instead, where we'd have more time to talk.

This was even more distressing. A private conference! I had never had an "audience" with a Catholic priest. How do I do this? Do you sit, do you stand, do you speak first or wait until he speaks. What if I do it all wrong. But the dream was so compelling and Father Pennington had seemed so compassionate. I had to take the chance.

Father's room was just down the hall, but my feet moved like they were in mud. I knocked lightly on the door, hoping he wouldn't hear. But the door opened.

"Come in, Helen."

Still I hesitated at the door. I said I didn't know what to do…I 'd never come to a priest for counsel before. His reassuring voice stilled my objections. "Just come sit down and we will visit awhile." He was so gracious, my fears diminished.

I poured out my story of the strange and penetrating experiences of this retreat — Mary's voice in the garden and the disturbing message that came from the warm depths of the Light.

Father listened with such quiet intensity. His reply was gentle but unequivocal.

"The Lord is asking you to forgive this man." Forgive him! This is impossible.

"<u>How</u>?" I managed to ask.

"Write him a letter."

He might just as well have told me to step out of the room, flap my arms, and fly to the moon! My thoughts tumbled around frantically.

"When?" I stammered.

"Today." Gentle and certain.

This is an inconceivable command. Impossible. Father doesn't know my story. He doesn't know this brutal murderer Mann has so many crimes on his hands, he'll be in prison forever. Surely it's best to let it be — for his sake.

"I don't even know what prison he's in!"

"Find out."

I said, "But my children....."

He said, "Give each a copy of your letter."

No! He doesn't know how John's death has strained us all to the breaking point. My children are already angry. If they knew I was writing the man who murdered their brother....

Very weakly I asked, "Oh, Father, isn't there an easier way? A book I could read on Forgiveness? I could pray for him. I'll pray every day that a prison chaplain, or someone trained for this, will help him."

"You don't need to read any more books, Helen. You know what to do."

My heart cried out inside me, " NO! I do <u>not</u> know!"

Father Pennington pressed on in his quietly relentless way, "There may not be enough humanity left in this man to understand your letter of forgiveness. But that's not your responsibility. You are doing this for <u>your</u> <u>own</u> <u>healing</u>. This is what God is asking of you."

How could I ever do this. How would I even begin. I'm nobody - a woman, alone and frightened by the words I'm hearing. Whatever happened to my restful retreat?

He spoke quietly of Jesus' own call to forgiveness and how He lived out that call in His own life. "Jesus is asking this of you because it is the only way out of your deepest grief." As I listened, I could feel the black hole, cold and bottomless at my core of my being. I was so tired of the years of bitter hatred and anger that weighed me down like a millstone.

He reminded me of Jesus' commandment to love others as He unfailingly loves us. He asked if I knew the Prayer of St. Francis. "Let me read it for you," he said. He opened his Bible. Inside the front cover he carried this prayer:

Lord, make me an instrument of Thy Peace.
> Where there is hatred, let me sow love.
> Where there is injury — pardon.
> Where there is doubt — faith,
> Where there is despair — hope,
> Where there is darkness — light,
> Where there is sadness — joy.
>> Divine Master, grant that I may not so much seek
>> to be consoled as to console,
>> to be understood as to understand,
>> to be loved as to love.
> For it is in giving that we receive. It is in pardoning that we are pardoned.
> And it is in dying that we are born to eternal Life.

Time seemed suspended. We stood up. I was still searching for other options, but held my tongue. Secretly I questioned the sanity of the direction. With a parting blessing, he said he would be praying for me, for my family, and for Gerald Mann.

It was the end of the retreat and we were saying good-byes. I didn't want to leave. I told Father Basil (no longer the formal name of Father Pennington after what we had shared) that a letter of forgiveness was beginning to form itself inside me.

"Send it on its way, Helen. Send it on its way," he said.

Home again, lonely, but reading to give myself a new understanding of Centering Prayer. It was this daily meditation that supported me as I began to draft the letter of forgiveness to Gerald Mann. I tentatively asked a few friends for their suggestions. They were encouraging, but could give no answers. I began to see that no one could do this except me.

Searching through the maze of judicial and government agencies, I was finally able to get the address of the institution where Gerald Mann was serving time, Atascadero State Hospital. I called and spoke with the chaplain there, Rev John Skelbred. When I told him I wanted to send a letter of forgiveness, he probably thought that I belonged in a state hospital too. He listened, though, and instructed me to send the letter unsealed, in a letter addressed to him. He assured me that he would personally coordinate this matter with the psychiatrist and social worker on Mann's case, and he would serve as my contact person at the prison.

It took a month to write that letter. Doubts often overshadowed faith as I wrote and re-wrote the sentences. Knowing that Father Pennington held me in his prayers kept me at my task, and finally, I had a draft that I could send without reservation.

First, copies of the letter went to my children. Agonized, I waited for their reactions; weeks later two responded. Some never did. All in all, the breach between us grew wider and the non-communication deepened. How much more lonely could I get!

What was my responsibility to my children now that they were grown? And what was my responsibility to my own restless spirit, longing to be healed.

It was time to mail the letter to Gerald Mann. As I approached the mailbox, total inertia weighed on me, slowing my steps. One hand held the letter, the other curved around the handle of the mailbox, completely unable to pull it down. How long did I stand there before grace propelled the letter into the slot?

That was it. I had followed all the instructions. I had done everything I had been asked to do.

June 23, 1988

Gerald Mann:

We have never spoken to one another. We do not know one another. Yet we have seen one another in the pain, the fear, the anger in the Marysville Court House. On June 3, 1980 you became a part of my life and hardly a day goes by without my memory bringing your name to my awareness. The days, weeks, months — from the date of your arrest on June 10, 1980 until the date of your sentencing on February 24, 1981 — I was in that courtroom each day you were there, for one of the many charges against you was the murder of my son John. The anger in your heart — the agony in mine forged a wall of steel and stone stronger than any prison ever built.

Eight years have passed — lonely, heartbreaking years for all of us — for me and for my family — as well as for you and for your family. Our Father in Heaven — your God and mine — for He created us both in His likeness and love — is asking me to allow Him to heal the wounds and to tear down the walls of anger that separate us. In the strength of our Lord I have been enabled to release John back to his Creator with prayers of thanksgiving for the 28 years I was allowed to be his mother and a part of his life.

Gerald, I cannot know the circumstances in your life which led you to such anger, fear, loneliness, emptiness, desperation. I can only know you must have seen the world and the people in it as your personal enemies.

It is time — for <u>all</u> of us — for the healing of scars and memories to begin. This kind of healing takes a lifetime, but it is possible for each one of us to understand that we can choose to live life in a new way — a healing and creating way. I choose this way for myself and will continually pray that you too will be able to choose your new way to live in our Father's forgiving love.

Gerald, I offer you my forgiveness just as our Lord Christ from His Cross on Calvary prayed to His Father and our Father:

"Father forgive them for they do not know what they are doing."

Gerald, since June 1980 you have been a part of my life. From June 1988 onward you will continue to be a part of my life but in a new, healing way. Every day, I promise, you will be in my daily, loving prayers for your healing and wholeness.

Helen Hansen

Such relief to have sent that letter. Such a sense of freedom. I could look back and see how each tentative step I had taken had been guided by a Love I cannot begin to understand. I know now that loving and compassionate help is always available to us, no matter how deeply mired we are in our own despair.

Without realizing it, Centering Prayer was becoming an integral part of my daily spiritual practice. In the deep silence, a Loving Father was at work clearing away old, useless mental debris and bringing into focus what was real and valuable in my life. The process was so gentle, so intelligent, I realized that I was in the hands of the consummate Therapist.

Memories of John began to return, no longer tormenting, but seemingly gentle, sunlit. A picture he had drawn of the Madonna and Child in delicate simple black lines, the softest shadings of forest green and gold brushed across the background. The Mother enfolds the Child, the Child is embracing the Mother. It's one of the few precious things of his I own. It seemed doubly beautiful to me now.

As John had traveled California, he had selected distinctive rocks for their uniqueness and quiet beauty, and used these to build a special wall in our front yard. He told me the history of every stone — its geological record and significance, where he had been camping when he found it. But I didn't write it down. I was going to write it down tomorrow, but that tomorrow never came. He placed each stone just so. One he set out a bit from the others so his little nieces would have a foothold. Their little feet found that step and took it to the top of the wall, where they sat and chatted like birds. John's wall was a deeply personal project that is his enduring gift to us.

And I remembered the last time John and I spoke. He had left so precipitously, setting out on the camping trip to parts unknown. Days and weeks had agonizingly gone by without hearing a word from him. Then that bright May morning — John's voice on the phone, clear, happy for the first time since coming home from war. He was calling from Wyoming. He spoke lyrically of the night skies full of stars and moon, and the sun shining on towering mountains rich the colors of new Spring. He said this trip had been a healing trip, truly healing. And he told me he loved me. How sweet those words were to remember. And he told me to tell everyone how much he loved them. He said that he would be seeing us all again in a little while. The last words from John were words of love.

Almost a year passed in this new freedom. I had done what Fr. Basil has asked – I had sent my letter and I prayed daily for Gerald Mann. I was getting on with my life at long last.

Then the letter came. It was from Gerald Mann. A letter saying he was sorry.

July 4, 1989

Helen E. Hansen:

You sent me a letter about a year ago. Your letter was a hard thing to deal with. It brought all my feelings out into the open and I had to face them and learn to deal with all the fear and anger.

I came to Atascadero State Hospital to get help for myself. I want to live with myself and not hide. It was a hard thing to do, coming here. Making the choice to deal with all the hatred, anger, fear, loneliness I feel. Then I got your letter. And coming to grips with all this and forgiving myself is the hardest thing. Your letter has made me cry and feel ashamed of myself. That is good for me because I have started to feel something other than anger and hatred. I have a long ways to go in my therapy here. And with my Dr.s help I want to. I want to be an ordinary person. Someday I will be a whole person. Thank you for helping me get the help I need. Your letter has helped me face the reality of what I have done.

Thank you for your forgiveness and your prayers. In my heart I know that I am sorry for taking John away from you. And you are right it is time for the healing to begin. It will take time maybe a lifetime. I do not know, but we have begun.

Gerald E. Mann

The prison chaplain, John Skelbred, phoned me just a few days later. He described how he had brought Gerald into the office and had given him my letter. He said Gerald had taken a long, long time looking at it — finally opening it, reading and re-reading it. It took him over an hour, trying to absorb my words and figure out what I meant. Finally, in a low noncommittal voice he said, "Tell her I'll write one letter and that will be the end of it."

Chaplain Skelbred urged me to come to Atascadero to meet with Gerald. He assured me that both he and the social worker would be in the same room with me. Would I come for one visit?

I took this troubling invitation into the silence of my Centering Prayer. Should I take this next step? The answer was clear and unequivocal. Yes.

You can guess the response of the prison administration to my request to visit the man who murdered my son. But, through the auspices of Chaplain Skelbred, permission was granted, and I set out for Atascadero. The 200-mile trek over highways and connecting routes provided time to think, and to pray. Meddlesome doubts rose up to plague me — What was I doing? And then I heard a voice inside, a voice I knew and loved — it was John's voice. I could scarcely believe it. So clear. He said, *"This is the way to go, Mom."*

Good as his word, Chaplain Skelbred met me when I arrived. As I began the security screening process at the front gate, I could not mistake the suspicious look from the officer in charge. Who was this woman identifying herself on the visitor register as "friend"? He asked to see my picture ID and told me to give him my purse for inspection and retention until the visit was over.

A very imposing scanning device with lights and buzzers loomed ahead.

"Just walk through," said the officer.

I walked through but the scanner rudely protested.

I backed out again.

"Remove your watch and ring."

I placed them on a wooden tray, walked through. Buzz. Failed.

"Remove your glasses and belt." BUZZZZ. Failed again.

"Remove your shoes."

My jangled nerves did not need this. As I stooped to remove my shoes, I muttered a protest to Moses, "Why should I remove my shoes? This isn't Holy Ground!"

But a voice resonated within me,

"This is Holy Ground, for here too I dwell."

Silenced, and in awed humility, I removed my shoes and walked through the scanner. It didn't make a sound.

Chaplain Skelbred led me through the bank of prison offices, into a large room with a one-way glass wall. I was given a seat at a small table. The social worker and psychiatrist sat nearby. A guard entered escorting the prisoner.

I had not seen Gerald Mann since the trial. Medium height, dressed in prison clothes, he glanced briefly at me and sat down directly across from me. Where would we begin? Gratefully, the social worker suggested Gerald begin by saying something about his life.

Never looking up, he spoke in a flat monotone, a report of a life both abusive and abusing. The lack of emotion or inflection made it seem as if he was talking about someone else's life, not his own. He came to the part about shooting my son. He threw me a glance and, in a strange, hollow tone asked, "Have you heard enough? Or do you want to hear some more?"

In the timeless pause that followed, a voice within me said,

"Don't be afraid. I am with you."

And then, my son's voice, speaking inside me again,

"This is the way to go, Mom!"

I heard myself say, "Continue with your story."

In that same lifeless tone, he said that John had owed him money. When he went to collect, John had come at him with a 2x4 and was threatening to kill him, so he shot in self-defense. It was so blatantly false, contradicting all the evidence. It was painfully difficult to listen.

I looked at Gerald's hands, clasped together so tightly that his fingers were white. This is the hand that held the gun that killed my son! At once a voice spoke in me:

"This is the hand of my broken child who does not know My Name."

I did not will it, but I found my open hand extending across the table to Gerald.

"Give me your hand, Gerald," my voice said.

He could not unclasp his fingers, but at last, with great effort, he pulled one hand free and dropped his fist heavily onto my palm. My fingers closed gently, holding his hand. His eyes, empty, vacant, were looking directly into mine.

"Gerald, there is nothing I can say or do that can change any part of your life, just as there is nothing you can say or do to change any part of mine. But I am here today to offer my forgiveness again. I believe we can always make new choices for living the rest of our lives. I choose to find healing from my anger, and I believe you have choices to change the way you think and react for the rest of your life." His vacant, staring eyes did not acknowledge that he had heard anything that I had said. In parting, I told him I would be praying for him and, I added, "Father Basil Pennington who guided me to write the letter of forgiveness is praying for both of us."

The visit was over. Gerald was taken back to his cell. In the lobby, the social worker enfolded me in her arms saying, "You are the most remarkable woman I've ever met." I asked her if she thought Gerald had heard anything I said. She assured me that he had heard every word. She said that this visit would give the hospital therapy team new leverage for working with Gerald to get past his cold exterior. I thought I saw a trace of tears in her eyes as she told me that she had read my forgiveness letter and knew of my sincerity it writing it. "I know this has been a deeply painful thing for you to do."

The long drive home after that first visit allowed time for all my fears to run riot. Who did I think I was, breaking into this man's horrible life with my bleating attempts at forgiveness? Where could all of this lead? Hadn't I already hurt my children too much? Foolish. Foolish . What if my crusade of forgiveness had created more problems for everyone? What would my husband have said? How much I missed him, needed him to guide me, to mirror back what was happening.

Who could I talk to? Who would even know what I was talking about? Father Basil was now halfway around the world, living in a monastery in Hong Kong. I didn't know his address. So, I did a most illogical thing. I turned to the back of my copy of *Open Mind, Open Heart* and found the address of its author. Father Thomas Keating had worked with Fr. Basil to bring Centering Prayer out of the monastery. In my letter I poured out my heart to him, describing all that had happened at the prison that day and the internal diatribes that had tormented me on the long drive home.

He replied, bless his heart. Faster than I thought my letter could have been received, he wrote back.

"Read again the story of Peter in his fishing boat when he saw Jesus walking across the water. The disciples all cried out, "It's a ghost!" Jesus spoke to them saying,

"Take heart. It is I. Have no fear."

Peter said in reply, "Lord, if it is you, command me to come to you on the water."

Jesus said, "Come."

Peter got out of the boat and began to walk on the water toward Jesus. But when he saw how strong the wind was, he became frightened and, beginning to sink, he cried out,

"Lord, save me!"

Immediately Jesus stretched out His hand and caught him. He said to him,

"O you of little faith. Why did you doubt Me?"

Fr. Thomas urged me to listen to Christ's voice calling me in faith to walk to Him across the turbulent waters. And he said something very poignant:

> when I had extended my hand to Gerald and enfolded his fist in my fingers, this was the Hand of God reaching out.

The infinite forgiveness of a Loving Father had begun to heal Gerald and me on that first visit at Atascadero.

Our second visit at Atascadero State Hospital was much more amiable. Both the social worker and the hospital chaplain had helped me understand Gerald's behavior. A sociopath shuts down all emotion, walls himself off from his feelings and those of his victims. He will re-interpret the facts about what happened, always justifying his actions by saying that the victim got just what he deserved. The invented story will become so firmly fixed in his own mind that he will tell it fifty times and not a word will have changed.

The staff had almost given up on Gerald. He was one of the angriest men they had ever seen, so withdrawn, so closed down despite therapy or any involvement in groups. They were unable to make even the smallest breakthrough. But after our first meeting, he began to relate to them. He was able to look directly into their eyes as they talked, and his overall demeanor had improved.

The chaplain brought me to his office. He insisted I take an alarm with me in case of emergency. But I felt no fear and promptly forgot I had it. When Gerald walked in with his counselor, he had a bit of a smile on his face. She mentioned almost in passing that "Gerry" had been thinking that maybe there is a God. Gerald said, "Yeah, and it's sort of exciting."

Gerald told me about being brought into the psychiatrist's office and given my letter. "All hell broke loose for me. I didn't know how to deal with it. It seemed to me I must have held your letter for an hour, reading it over and over, trying to understand the words from the mother of one of my victims......his name was John. Helen, none of the people I hurt had names.

"Dr Slater told me I <u>had</u> to meet you because, if I didn't, I would always wonder who this woman was. Who would write me a letter forgiving me for taking the life of her son? Helen, you will never understand how hard...how painful it was. After the trial, I never wanted to see you again."

He said the therapist kept "working on him" to write his response to me, making him re-write it four times before he would mail it. Four times! It must have been a painful struggle for him just to write it the first time.

"When I actually met you I was scared to death. When you reached your hand over and I put my hand in yours, it was such a shock – I tried with all my strength, mental and physical, to pull it away – but it wouldn't move. Something like a tight cord wrapped around my fist holding it so I couldn't take it back. Your hand was so tender, gentle, as if my fist wasn't really touching, but resting on a layer of air."

We both agreed it was not a human power that held our hands in place. This memory is still very significant for both of us.

"Your letter and your visit played right into the doctor's hands. He wouldn't let me get by with my usual refusals to answer any more. Now, he gets right in my face and almost shouts, 'That's bull-shit! You know it and I know it. Now let's try this again.' " Gerald said that no one had ever made him take a hard look at his life of destructive actions before.

Near the end of the visit we stood up, the chaplain and the counselor stepped out into the hall and left us alone together for a few moments. We were both comfortable. I felt safe. I said, "Gerald, before I leave, I would like to give you a hug, so you might know the embrace of a mother's love." It was a fragile moment for me, knowing his background.

He replied without hesitation, "Yeah. I'd like that."

We embraced, firmly, warmly. It was entirely right, holding one another, and healing for us both. He returned to the darkness of prison life and I to the freedom of the highway and home.

One morning not long after, I was deep in Centering Prayer.

Tears were pouring from my eyes because I had heard,

"I am giving you a son."

Everything in me cried back, "Not this son! You took away the son I loved and You are giving me this man I hated to be my son!"

Quite unexpectedly, my tears stopped, replaced by a peaceful, quiet knowing:

"Yes, a son to love....a son in Spirit."

Gerald had begun to change. Working with the psychiatrist and staff, he had become a cooperative participant in his own therapy. He has an additional burden to face — he has a terminal illness, an inherited polycystic kidney disease that runs in his family. A kidney transplant is not an option for him; he will probably die before his sentence expires.

Gerald and the medical staff agreed that the time had come for him to leave the hospital and be assigned to a prison to live out the term of his sentence. He was moved to Soledad State Prison.

I wrote for permission to continue my visits with Gerald, even though Soledad was some distance from Sacramento. An official letter informed me that the mother of a murdered victim would never be allowed into the prison to visit an inmate. My first thought was, well, that's it then. I've done everything I could, even more than Fr. Basil had asked. The prison officials have made my decision for me.

But Spirit said,

"Not so fast. Write another letter."

So I wrote another letter. This time the Warden authorized limited, "non-contact visitor" status; we would visit with a glass barrier between us and converse through telephone receivers.

My first visit was a bureaucratic disaster. I had been instructed to arrive at the visitor center at 12:30; I was there at 12:15. My letter from the warden seemed to carry no authority with the staff because they did not have a copy of their own.

"Did anyone tell you that you could not be processed at the visitor center until 1:45?"

"No, I was instructed to be here by 12:30."

"Mann is on work assignment. If an inmate has a work assignment, he cannot be excused until after he finishes work. Then, if he has a visitor, he must shower and clean up before he can visit."

"Mr Mann does have a work assignment but he had submitted the paperwork to his supervisor who signed permission for Mr Mann to be released from work for this day."

The lady officer stated adamantly that no inmate is ever permitted to be released from work detail. All visits had to be after work. Another officer said that I could stay late - visiting hours were over at 8 PM.

I replied that, as I didn't drive at night, I would not be able to stay that late.

I sat and waited for two hours. What else could I do? Finally, an officer called me to the desk, apologized for the delay saying that they had found their copy of the warden's directive. She processed me through the security screening and directed me to the visiting area.

There I waited thirty minutes until Gerald was escorted into his side of the glass booth. We picked up our phones and began our first non-contact visit. It seemed so strange to interact through this artificial barrier to our new acquaintance. But we managed. Just thirty minutes later, the guard was at my side saying the visit was over.

The second visit, two months later, was even more provoking. When I arrived Monday afternoon at the Soledad visiting center, I was informed that they had discontinued visitation on Mondays. The fact that I had the warden's permission to visit him in my hand did not help. I told them that I had driven from Sacramento, that I had cleared this date and time with the prison counselor's office, that Gerald's supervisor had approved his work release for this day, and that he was expecting me to visit. They would not relent and there was no recourse but to make the four-hour drive back home and write Gerald. His letter in return said that he had waited in his cell all day, no one had informed him that Mondays had been canceled, and he was very disappointed not to have seen me.

My impression is that the lines of communication between the prison's administration offices and front-line duty personnel are woefully inadequate. They seem to have no interest whatever in prisoners receiving visitors. One could argue: why should they? Why should a murderer have <u>any</u> human comfort extended to him? This attitude assumes: once a criminal, always a criminal. All hope for redemption is negated. His monstrous acts have set him squarely outside of humanity forever. By his own choosing. I believed this myself at one time.

But, as I read it, this is completely overturned by the Gospels. Jesus never gives up on anyone. His forgiveness has no exceptions. His love and example are all about re-humanizing us and He leaves no one out. This is what was happening to Gerald and me. In some mysterious, grace-filled way, my visits with Gerald were essential to healing us both.

Some months later, as I drove through the valley, over the coastal range, into the prison parking lot, my heart was full of grateful prayer. I was asking God to prepare the way for our visit.

We had over four hours together. I asked Gerald about his childhood. He said that he didn't have such a bad childhood. His happiest memories were of fishing with his older brother, or camping in the woods with friends, or exploring. He and his brother loved exploring abandoned gold miners' caves, finding old whiskey bottles, miners' tools, and rusted tin cans. One old can still had flakes of gold in it. They found a cave where the owner had carved his bed out as a ledge in the wall, the perfect hideout to safeguard his treasure.

Only when I asked him to remember what was best in his childhood had these memories resurfaced. He spoke wistfully about how much he missed that — his love of nature and the freedom to roam and explore wherever he wanted. His face lit up as he remembered riding his 10-speed bike through the mountains of Northern California. A special memory was Lassen Volcanic National Park with its hot, bubbling lava pots emitting earth's sulfur fumes. An amazing 60-ton boulder perches precariously on its ledge, once part of the inside of the mountain before being blasted out by the unimaginable force of the volcano. He said he felt most alive when he was out biking alone in the mountains.

Gerald said he didn't really know where it had all gone wrong.

He had some good memories of his family, yet he said that, as a child, he often felt that he didn't belong. His self-image was of an unwanted child in hand-me-down clothes. Early on, he began to act out his feeling of being rejected. With every lashing out and its punitive consequence, he withdrew more and more from everyone, even those who might have cared, if he had given them the chance. He was a troubled kid that nobody knew what to do with. Now he remembers with deep regret his hostility toward his family, and all the hurt he caused them. In his imprisoned loneliness, he misses them very much.

We talked about the hospital diagnosis of sociopath. He said he never thought of himself that way, except in his younger days, when he really wondered at times if he was crazy. We talked about the definition of sociopath — "a psychopathic personality whose behavior is aggressively anti-social" — someone who has no sense of self worth or of the value of any other humans.

Gerald said that pretty well described who he was. His violence against others became more and more out of control. He said the prison psychiatrist had helped him understand that there was an addiction to violence, an excitement in hurting people. He added that so many were in prison because of the same thing — the excitement of stealing a car to see if they can get away with it. He said this was common prison conversation. Stealing, rape, home burglaries, killing ...the excitement of the action. He didn't plan what would happen ahead of time. He would get up in the morning and say, "Something exciting is going to happen today." And whoever he met that day would be the victim.

Hearing this, I felt my whole body grow clammy and cold. Somehow I managed to ask,

"Do you mean...are you saying my son's life meant no more to you that day than....the day's excitement?"

Again I heard within,

"Don't be afraid. I am with you."

And again, John's clear voice,

"This is the way to go, Mom."

Gerald's barely audible answer was, "Yeah."

Only with God's strength was I able to remain calm during the remainder of our visiting time that day and able to express my love for him as I left.

I got into my car completely numb, refusing to acknowledge the wave of emotion that threatened to overwhelm me. Night was falling, thunderclouds were gathering overhead, mirroring the growing turmoil in my heart. Lightning flashes brought a torrential downpour and my heart gave way to torrential tears. A tidal wave of grief overtook me, flooding my vision, wrenching sobs from my deepest being on the long, long drive home. How did I ever arrive safely? I can not tell you. I pulled into my garage and literally fell across the steering wheel in complete exhaustion.

Then it happened.

A great wave of powerful energy rolled through me, over me, washing away all the years of hot, grimy, hate-encrusted tears. In its wake, a warm and soft peacefulness, so deep and still, undefinable, came to rest in me. It became the indelible center of my being, closing up and healing forever the cold black hole that had been my constant companion.

That Peace has never left me in all the years since.

For over ten years of prison visits now, Gerald and I have shared our stories, both starting from our very similar prisons of hate. An unforgiving angry Christian and angry atheist sociopath — what an impossible start. As our friendship has matured, I've discovered that Gerald too, has a soul longing to be healed and set free. He told me that he believes more and more that there may be a God, although he can't understand Him. And he speaks of his soul, our souls, finding our way together.

He remembers and appreciates all that his doctors and counselors did for him. He knows they cared about him as a person. He quotes them with great respect, remembering their words that continue to bring him new and deeper insights. Each time we visit, Gerald states that he has only himself to blame for his bad choices. He doesn't blame anyone in his family, he doesn't blame society. He says he earned the right to be in prison. Yet always, he longs for the freedom he will never know again on earth.

He has discovered his wonderful gift for calligraphy and artwork, as you can see from this book's beautiful cover. His design for my beloved St. Francis Prayer of Peace hangs here over my desk, written in rich blue script. On one side he has drawn a blue-green hummingbird with my name and a phoenix bird with his name on the other.

Prayer For Peace

Lord, make me an instrument
    of Your peace.
Where there is hatred...
    let me sow love.
Where there is injury... pardon,
Where there is doubt... faith,
Where there is despair... hope,
Where there is darkness... light,
Where there is sadness... joy,

Lord, grant that I may seek rather
    to comfort than be comforted,
To understand rather than to
    be understood,
To love than to be loved.
For it is by giving that one receives,
By forgiving that one is forgiven,
And by dying that one awakens
    to eternal life.

Helen

Gerald

Gerald has been suffering for many years from his kidney disease. Now his kidneys are failing and he is facing a dependency on kidney dialysis. Soon he will be transferred to a prison medical facility where he will be undergoing dialysis three or four times a week, each session three hours in duration.

What a long way Gerald has come — all the way back from a sub-human existence to claim his true Self as child of God. From the thank you letters Gerald wrote to Father Basil and Father Thomas:

"I lost my way for a lot of years. Years of hate and anger. I hurt a lot of people. I just did not care. Then Helen wrote me a letter forgiving me. It was the hardest letter I have ever read. It made me cry and I got angry and wanted to hurt someone. And it took me a whole year to write Helen back.

"Helen was able to break through to me with three words. "I forgive you."

It turned my world upside down. I learned what those words meant. I did it the hard way. I experienced shame, fear, anger, hate, and loneliness. I did not like what I saw in myself. So I worked hard, through a lot of tears, to find my way. And when I learned to communicate my feelings to others, I was able to write Helen back – and to communicate with her. Then I learned to forgive myself and then to find a new me — one I like a lot."

Forgiveness does not come naturally. It is completely counterintuitive to our most righteous beliefs. But Fr. Basil taught me that, even if the offender never responds, I had to offer him forgiveness for my own healing to begin.

I look back with humility and gratitude for the loving guides, Father Basil and Father Thomas, sent to me on this incredible journey. As Gerald said in one of his letters,

"They are 'Angels of Love'. Without them we would be lost. God spoke to them and they in turn spoke to you and you spoke to me — so you would not lose your way and for you to help me, a lost soul, to find my way back to God's arms."

In all of our visits now we are separated by a glass partition, speaking to each other through plastic telephone receivers. At the close of each visit, the guard gives us a three-minute warning that time is about up. In that last parting moment, I would place my hand on the window separating us, and through the phone I would say, "Gerald, I believe in a God of incredible mercy Who longs for the healing of all His children." For many of the first visits, he would glance at my hand and then tell me to be careful on the drive home; he didn't want anything to happen to me. After a time though, he would momentarily touch his hand on his side of the glass partition as he left. Then, at the end of one visit, when I placed my hand on the glass, he placed his hand to match mine on his side and kept it there. It became our parting pledge of love for one another. This is a love like no other I have ever known. It is God's Love speaking through us and healing us.

Every time I go into Centering Prayer, I take Gerald into my heart with me, knowing that Abundant Love is reaching out to both of us. Victims no more! Gerald and I are now enfolded in the wonder, the mystery, and the infinite power of God to heal and restore all He has created.

I sent Gerald a copy of this manuscript before it was published; after all, it is his story too. He wrote back:

Dear Helen;

I just received a copy of your book. I read it through one time. I thought I would write and let you know.

It is a very powerful peace of writing. I did not like all the memories that came back to me while I read it. I knew they would but I did not think they would be so strong. I feel so much shame after reading it. And that is good for me because it reminds me just how far I have come and how far I have to go.

Helen my first thought was "Gerald do not change any thing in the book about you. Because it is all true." That is what I want to be told. The Truth. I do not want to hide from it.

Helen you do have a way with words. You got right to the point and stayed there. It was easy to understand. It was very moving and brought tears to my eyes. God gave you a gift Helen. God also gave me a very special gift too. You, Helen E. Hansen. I thank God every day now for that. Because you gave me back myself. And of course Dr. Slater and Donna helped me.

Faith, trust, love and caring are more than just simple words. I found out what they really do mean.

I sure do hope that our story will help someone. I would like to know what Fr. Pennington and Fr. Keating have to say after reading our story.

I want to get this out to you tonight. I am going to read the book again. I will write in a couple of days.

Take care. And well done Helen.

Love Your Friend
Gerald

And later he wrote:

Dear Helen;

About your book. First off let me say I do love the book. It was truthful and to the point. I do not want to change any part about me. It is the truth. I can not hide from it nor do I want too.

I knew that reading it would bring back a lot of bad memories for me. And the strongest emotion I had was guilt. I ruined a lot of lifes for what I thought was a good high. And boy was I wrong.

I was a very angry young man. My hate controled my every thought and everything I did. I could blame other people for the way I acted and felt. But that would have been a lie. I and I alone am responsible for my actions. If I blame my family or other people then that would be just a cop-out. I will not do it.

Helen you came to me in 1988 with 3 words "I forgive you". Those were hard words to read and to bear. They changed my life. And thanks to you Helen I was forced to make a choice. 1) To routine my old behavior and live a life of hate and anger. 2) Or change and fess-up to what I was and work to better myself. I wanted to feel the guilt. I had to learn to feel emotion again. I had to cry and feel real pain deep inside of myself. Otherwise I would not change any thing. And I can say this, it was not easy at all. And it is still hard some times. All the anger, fear, pain, and the loneliness I felt while I went through this experience was well worth it to me. I got to meet one of the most courageous women in the world. You

Helen gave me the courage and strength to face my fears and pain of changing.

Your book is a work of art Helen. Good job. Your book will help others. And like me it will help other come back into the LORD's arms. I did and I am a better person for it. It feels good.

Love Your Friend,
Gerald

Postscript

I recently spoke to prisoners at Folsom State Prison. In a letter of thanks, one of the men wrote:

"It's the worst of sinners who feels that he or she is unforgivable, who is incapable of self-forgiveness. We've long since lost all hope of ever being forgiven by society and accept that we will be despised forever by humankind. Helen's message operates on a profoundly personal level. She makes one realize the possibility that the people we have victimized might forgive us. For many of us this realization comes with the force of a revelation.

Helen's message of forgiveness is absolutely crucial for those who have never had examples of forgiveness in their lives — who, cut off from the world by concrete walls, will never have access to those they've offended and so never have a chance to ask for their forgiveness.

Perhaps you find it offensive that criminals should forgive themselves. Perhaps you believe that people convicted under the Law *should*, in fact, drag around a permanent burden of guilt until the day they die. But the great majority of people now in prison will be paroled one day. Unless something has changed in that person, whatever it was that brought them to prison will persist. By wishing permanent punishment, you condemn these people, and yourself, to continued victimization.

There are profound social implications for the prisoner who discovers self-forgiveness and there are profound social implications for the victim of crime who discovers forgiveness (rather than vengeance).

I was deeply grateful that Helen brought us her warmth and compassion and example of forgiveness. But it's significance need not stop at the merely personal, just as Jesus' Gospel was never intended to apply only to the individual. This "miracle" is available to everyone.

Michael